T0171569

Stopping the Epidemic of Divorce

Practical steps to stop divorce in its tracks

BARRY COOPER

WESTBOW
PRESS
A DIVISION OF THOMAS NELSON

Copyright © 2012 by Barry Cooper.

All rights reserved. No part of this book may be used or reproduced by any means, graphic, electronic, or mechanical, including photocopying, recording, taping or by any information storage retrieval system without the written permission of the publisher except in the case of brief quotations embodied in critical articles and reviews.

WestBow Press books may be ordered through booksellers or by contacting:

WestBow Press
A Division of Thomas Nelson
1663 Liberty Drive
Bloomington, IN 47403
www.westbowpress.com
1-(866) 928-1240

Because of the dynamic nature of the Internet, any web addresses or links contained in this book may have changed since publication and may no longer be valid. The views expressed in this work are solely those of the author and do not necessarily reflect the views of the publisher, and the publisher hereby disclaims any responsibility for them.

Any people depicted in stock imagery provided by Thinkstock are models, and such images are being used for illustrative purposes only.

Certain stock imagery © Thinkstock.

ISBN: 978-1-4497-3895-2 (hc)
ISBN: 978-1-4497-3894-5 (sc)
ISBN: 978-1-4497-3896-9 (e)

Library of Congress Control Number: 2012901621

Printed in the United States of America

WestBow Press rev. date: 02/27/2012

Contents

This book is dedicated to my wonderful daughter
and son-in-law,

Who have been there when the times were rough and
have given me two wonderful grandsons

Preface

I was married to a beautiful wonderful woman where we share great memories of thirty years.

I recognize that her memories of the events described in this book are different than my own. She is a fine, decent and hard-working woman. The book was not intended to hurt my friends or ex-wife. Both my publisher and I regret any unintentional harm resulting from the publishing and marketing of "*Stopping the Epidemic of Divorce.*"

How it Began

In 2008 and early 2009, even into 2010, there were worries about the bird flu and the swine flu. This was to be the worst disaster of the modern world. The flu was predicted to be a worldwide pandemic where thousands of people would be hospitalized and over half would lose their lives. The flu was going to have devastating effects on the world. The workforce would be cut by a third and be out sick for several weeks. The world and the healthcare system would not look the same after it was over.

I work as a Paramedic, and we had meetings on how we would be affected and how we could protect ourselves. It was predicted that a third of our workforce would be out and our call volume would double. It was going to be a very tough task to overcome. It would be devastating at times till the waves would pass. People were getting vaccines and inoculations to help prevent the upcoming disaster. By the grace of God, none of the bad things happened, only a few people were sick, they were isolated from the population, and the crisis was averted.

It was a horrible time for me; I was going through a divorce from a marriage of thirty years. It was a very dark time in my life. I had a lot of time on my hands and began drawing parallels between what was happening in my life to what was going on in the world. I realized that the real plague on humanity had become divorce. It has caused more pain and sorrow than the flu ever thought about causing. It has changed lives forever. It has a far-reaching effect, even down to second and third generations. More than half of the marriages today end in divorce. Homes are wrecked, and children are left without fathers or mothers. It is a sad day for humanity. What are we doing about it? There are no meetings, no planning, and no thoughts of how to deal with this growing problem, yet more than half of us will go through it! When is the plague going to stop? When is the pandemic on the family going to come to an end? What is the cure? Can it be stopped?

The Disease Process

God did a wonderful job when he made us and formed us. He patterned us after himself. He knew what he was doing. He had it worked out, even down to a cellular level. The disease process is very complicated and goes down to a microscopic level. I am in no way qualified to explain it at that level, but here's the simple version. The disease process is a set process that takes place no matter what the stimulus. When we are exposed to bacteria or a virus, the process is the same. The stimulus is the bacteria or virus, and it gets in the body by several means: ingesting, breathing, or even absorbing through the skin. How the stimulus gets in is important, but not as important as to what happens once it is in the body. This stimulus is called an antigen in the body. The body recognizes it as a foreign substance and moves it to an isolated area. The body then studies it and figures out what to do with it. It is carried to the lymph nodes to be studied. Once the body figures out that it is indeed a foreign substance, white blood cells come in and surround it and kill it. They do this by destroying themselves. They kill themselves to kill the antigen. If it is too much for the white blood cells, the body calls in reinforcements called histamines. Histamines are toxic to the antigen and also have effects on our bodies. They can cause us to have runny noses and lots of coughing. This is an attempt to rid the body of the antigen. If the histamines are unsuccessful, the foreign body overcomes the body's defenses and will soon overtake it. The body becomes sick and could die if not treated. I know this is very rudimentary, and the body is much more complex than this, but you will see parallels to this process and the death of the marriage.

When you go to work and someone catches your eye or you go to Web sites that you know you don't need to or you go places that your spouse doesn't know you are going, this is the antigen—the foreign body or stimulus. These things happen a lot and could even take place every day. These are not uncommon. It is what you do with the stimulus that is the deciding factor: if you allow it to become a stimulus, if you just turn your head and not linger at the pretty person, or if you just say no and don't go where you know you shouldn't be in the first place, the stimulus is reduced to nothing and doesn't grow. The stimulus is killed. If you give it space and start to rationalize it in your mind or if you think about it, it will grow. If you say, "Just this one time," or "No one will ever know," you are heading for big trouble. "One time" will be followed by "it was okay the last time I did it," and it will become easier to do it the next time and the next time—it is growing. You then isolate this behavior to a certain side of yourself, the side not even your spouse knows about. You hide the behavior and keep it secret. This side of you becomes a part of who you are. This stimulus, if not treated, will overcome you. In your mind, you think about it and start to rationalize your behavior. You start making time for it. You make room for it in your life. You might hide it for a while, but there is someone that knows all about you and your behavior, someone you can't hide it from. God knows about it and calls it sin. God is the white blood cells. He comes in and surrounds you and convicts your soul. He also surrounds you with his love, and it hurts him for you to sin. He provides an out for you, but he lets you make that choice. He tries to isolate you from your sin.

1 Corinthians 10:13 (*New King James Version*) "No temptation has overtaken you except such as is common to man: but God is faithful who will not allow you to be tempted beyond what you are able, but with the temptation will also make the way of escape, that you may be able to bear it."

He even does as white blood cells do; he died to take you away from the sin you are committing. He covers you and protects you from the evil antigen. God gives us an out, a way to not choose the temptation. So many times we don't take his out, we most often choose the sin and ignore the way out he has provided. We are too wrapped up in the sin. We feed it and watch it grow; sometimes it makes us happy and feels good, when we get into the sin, even though Christ died to keep us from it! Stop and think about that for a second. Christ died to keep us from it, but we feed it and watch it grow. *Wow!*

If it keeps growing and our stimulus gets more embedded in our lives, God allows the toxic effects to have consequences over us. Just as the histamine is released in our bodies and floods our systems, the consequences flood our lives. God allows us to have these things to help us understand that we are doing wrong, and that, despite the fact that we are doing wrong, he still loves us and wants us to do the right things.

Some of the consequences that come into our lives are small at first, but they, too, grow bigger. It may start as more arguments with our spouses or finding fault with them. We start looking for things they are doing wrong, and this emasculates the man and causes the women to feel unloved. This behavior feeds our stimuli and helps us justify our wrong behaviors. For men, it may start as small comments like:

"She doesn't have sex with me."

"I can't remember the last time we had sex."

Or women might say:

"You never take out the trash."

"You never help me around the house."

"You never help me with the kids."

"You never do anything I ask you to do."

These comments start out small and subtle but could grow and become more and more prevalent. This whole process does nothing more than put the spouse down and feed our stimuli. We then start to feel comfort in our sin, and it doesn't feel like we are doing anything wrong. It becomes a bigger part of us, and it will soon overcome us. Once it consumes us, death is right around the corner. Not the death of a living human, but the death of a relationship and possibly the death of the family. Don't be fooled into thinking that death of the family doesn't have an effect on anyone but the spouses. It will affect the kids whether they are grown and have families of their own or not. It will affect our workplaces. It will affect our parents, brothers, and sisters. It will even have an effect on the church we attend on a regular basis. People don't know what to say. They don't want to appear to take sides. Friends will move away from us. The children bear the brunt of the effects of the death of the marriage. You need to know this: you might think your small little sin, the one tucked away in that small little place that no one knows about, will grow and be brought out in the open for everyone to see. It will grow to be bigger than life. It just needs the right food in order to grow and consume you and leave a path of destruction behind.

Proverbs 16:25 "There is a way that seems right to a man But its end is the way of death."

Proverbs 19:23 "The fear of the Lord leads to life and he who has it will abide in satisfaction: He will not be visited with evil."

The Immune System and Genetics

Anyone who follows any sport will know that the best defense is a good offence. The immune system works under that same principle. If you have a good immune system, your body will be able to fight off foreign invaders. The body will destroy the invader. This is also true in our marriages. If you have a healthy, strong marriage, it will be able to withstand a lot of pain and wrongdoings. If the marriage is healthy and strong, the spouse will be able to avoid the temptation of other men and women. If the marriage is not strong, thoughts of infidelity may begin to invade the spouse's thoughts. Take Bill and Jane for an example. They had just moved into the neighborhood. They had seen several people walking and some running through the neighborhood. Bill decided to start exercising. He began by walking. He would often invite Jane for an evening walk. Most of the time she was just too tired from working all day and it was a hassle with the kids. So she would tell him to go without her. On his walks he would often see Diane walking. He would see her quite often and would do the neighborly thing and strike up a conversation. Soon they would plan their walks at the same time. It was all innocent till one day Diane had a bad day at work and was feeling down. Diane was very upset and just didn't feel like walking. So they spent their walk time at her house drinking coffee. This is how things start out completely innocent and then move quickly to not a good choice. Those thoughts will occupy a lot of space in the mind. This stimulus doesn't have to be someone at work or at a restaurant; it can be a television program, book, or maybe even pornography. I know you are asking yourself how pornography or other distractions can affect a marriage. Well, it gets in the mind and you began to compare the pictures to your spouse. You will begin to think about what the pictures or movies are acting out. You will then begin to seek out harder and more outlandish movies or pictures. Then you will start thinking that these images represent normal behavior and that something is wrong with my spouse because they won't behave the same way. This will lead you down a path of destruction, the path we talked about in the previous chapter—the path that leads to the death of the marriage.

Romans 13:13, 14: "Let us walk properly as in the day. Not in revelry and drunkenness, not in lewdness and lust, not in strife and envy. But put on the Lord Jesus Christ, and make no provision for the flesh to fill its lust."

Another factor in the immune system is genetics. It plays a factor in how our bodies react. You are now wondering how genetics plays a factor in a marriage. Well, it doesn't play much of a factor unless you have children. Sometimes genetic factors cause our children to be born with birth defects. (Boy that sounds very harsh.) If you don't think having a child with developmental problems doesn't put a strain on the marriage, then you are not thinking straight. I'm sure one or the other parent feels like it is his or her fault. If this is the case, you need to get that thought out of your head right now! God placed that little one in your trust and care for a reason. If you abandon the love for the child or the spouse that helped create that bundle of love, the marriage will certainly suffer. Both parents need to be mindful that God put you together, and he also put this bundle of love in your life. You need to step up to the challenge and stick it out. Enjoy the job that God has placed before you. Without a doubt, you will initially feel wronged and want to point fingers. You need to put that behavior behind you and work through those feelings and accept the job. Joy will certainly come. It may not be as you envisioned, but it will come.

I have a great friend that has a child with a learning disability. He has often said that his other children would come to him and say, "Look, Daddy, I got an A on my paper today." His other child would come to him and say, "Daddy I scored the most points in the game today." His dear child with a learning disability would come to him and say, "Daddy I learned to tie my shoe today." As a parent, you need to celebrate all accomplishments, big and small. What you might see as small may be big from a different perspective. You need to celebrate your children's accomplishments. Bitterness is caused by unmet expectations. We will explore this in greater detail later. Both bitterness and individual expectations play a huge factor in the strength of a marriage.

Another potential cause of stress in a marriage has nothing to do with genetics. It is learned behaviors. Being raised in the South, I was brought up on foods like fried chicken and fried pork chops. These were served often with mashed potatoes and green beans. Of course these are high fat meals and are not considered healthy. If a young girl left the house to get married and couldn't cook a least biscuits or cornbread, people thought her mother didn't do a good job of raising her. When I got married, this was the type of food I expected; I didn't know anything different. It was a learned lifestyle. If you were brought up in a stressful or controlling household, this could shape your expectations for your own marriage. Not to mention sexual or physical abuse. These will certainly cause problems in a marriage. Obviously these are extremes. However, subtle behaviors or past experiences can be subtle, like how strict your parents were when you were growing up, or if children in your family were expected to play sports. As a boy in the South, you were either a linebacker or quarterback. The question was not whether or not you wanted to play football but what position you wanted to play.

My son-in-law had to work one night. This is a rare occasion, so I, being the great dad that I am, took a pizza to my daughter's house to have supper with my grandson and daughter. We sat and ate supper. I noticed my grandson pulling off the pepperonis. I was surprised: what kid doesn't like pepperoni? He pulled all of them off and basically only ate a cheese pizza. I thought that was odd. My daughter and I were making a big dent in the other pizza, which was piled high with everything but the kitchen sink. My son-in-law was getting ready for work at the time and came out of the shower. Before leaving, he stopped and got a slice of pizza. Guess what he did? Yes, he took off the pepperoni. Do you think my grandson doesn't like pepperoni, or do you think that he takes it off because his Dad does? He was only two years old. I don't think he knew if he liked pepperoni or not, but that is what he has seen his dad do, and that is what he thinks you should do with pizza. This is another example of learned behavior. Think about things you do. Why do you do them? Do you squeeze the toothpaste from the bottom up, or do you squeeze the tube until something comes out? When you wash your car, do you start at the top then wash the hood and trunk, and then the rest of the car? How did you learn to wash the car? Does it matter how you wash it? Some people have set ways of doing things. In the long run, does it really matter how something is done?

Much of my career in the fire service was spent on a unit called the Squad. This unit had all the heavy extrication tools aka—the Jaws of Life. My job was to cut people out of cars after accidents. Once promoted, I moved to a Command vehicle and had different responsibilities. It was very hard for me to not grab the tools and cut the car. Cutting cars was now someone else's job. He was well trained and was very good at doing it. That didn't keep me from wanting to tell him how to do it, or even taking the tools from him and doing it myself. I had to learn a lesson that has served me well since then: that as long as we come to the same ending point, it doesn't matter how we get there.

I say this to bring home the fact that in a marriage, your spouse is going to do things differently than you do, but as long as you get the same results, don't sweat the little things.

Of course, there might be better ways of doing things. If you let the small things go and look for the end result, you will build up your spouse and gives him or her feelings of empowerment. It tells your spouse that you trust him or her. If you praise the end result, (ignoring how the task was accomplished). You will empower your spouse.

For example, did your father help your mother clear the table and do the dishes? Or did he go in the living room and watch *Sports Center*? Imagine that your father always helped with the dishes, and you've just married a man whose father never helped with the dishes. His dad went in the living room and left the "woman's work" to his wife. What types of conflicts do you imagine in this new marriage? Sure, this issue of household work can be addressed over time. Will it ever be worked out fully? I am not saying that marriages fail because men don't help out in the kitchen. However, if the woman does not share her expectations that her husband help with the dishes, this could lead to resentment. Resentment will lead to bitterness. Bitterness will certainly harm and could even destroy a marriage if it goes untreated.

Both genetics and learned behaviors play a huge factor in a marriage. They are not easily overcome and take a lot of patience, kindness, and hard work to address. A lot of people don't take the time to work out these differences. They give up too quickly. Marriage is a long compromise that is filled with love and affection for the partner God has given you. Your spouse is not there by chance: he or she was put there by God to give you a helper. In Genesis, it says that God gave Adam a helper, not a wife. You spouse is your helper: someone that helps you through tough times, someone to celebrate with you. A strong marriage is like a strong immune system. Tempting thoughts are crushed. These thoughts don't lead to action.

I had a pastor friend that said that men are very visual creatures. If a pretty woman walks in a room or within 100 feet of a man, he will notice her. Men are genetically drawn to look. They can't stop from looking. How long they look is up to them. Do they look at her and then turn away? Or do they watch her every move? This could be called leering. This is the behavior that gets in the mind and causes problems. Leering can lead some men to lust. A strong marriage and a healthy relationship will help the man look away. It will help him overcome this natural instinct.

Signs and Symptoms

I feel that God gives us small clues or hints of things that are about to take place. These clues help you know what might be coming next. I call these signs and symptoms. In the medical field, we know that signs are things that you see, like a cut finger or a broken arm. In a marriage, it is not easy to see the signs. For example, when you see a dark cloud approaching, you start thinking rain is on the way. You start listening for thunder and watching for lightning. When you see the wind starting to pick up and hear thunder, you have certain expectations about what will happen next. These expectations come from past experiences. You start looking for shelter and you gather your things. You get the children to a safe place to protect them. These behaviors have helped us to weather the storms in the past. God does the same thing in our marriages. We just need to know the signs and learn what we need to do to weather the storm. We will *all* go through the storm at some time in our marriages.

Notice I didn't say *if* we go through the storm, but *when*. The old principles that what doesn't kill you makes you stronger are almost true. What's missing is the knowledge that God and his help keeps you safe. He lifts you up out of the danger and keeps you from dying. God puts all of us in a safe place to weather the storm.

I saw a lot of signs and symptoms in my marriage. I knew the marriage was struggling. I didn't know what to do. I could see the storm cloud building, but I didn't know what to do next. I relied on God a lot and I prayed. The apostle Paul says to pray without ceasing. (**1 Thessalonians 5:17**). I know all about that—my mind was fully consumed with the brewing problem. Still, I didn't know what to do. I did the only thing I knew, which was to become, in my mind, "the perfect husband." My wife had a job out of town, an hour commute each way. This turned her days into ten-hour days, five days a week. I was working twenty-four hours on and forty-eight hours off at the fire department. Therefore, two out of the three days, I was home waiting on her. I would start supper before she got home. I greeted her at the door and had a bath ready when she came in. She would get in the bubble bath and I would kneel down next to the tub and we would talk about her day. This was her time. I did this every night I was home. I was only doing what I thought she wanted in a husband. I was trying to become "the perfect husband." She was tired, and I was trying to do everything to make her life easier. This went on for close to a year. I didn't know what else to do. I was trying to provide her with a safe, welcoming, and pampered life. Our relationship with God is similar to this. You can't work your way into heaven. All the work you do is not good enough. God doesn't want a so-called slave; he wants a relationship. I was trying to work my way back into my wife's heart, I didn't know how to give her anything but what I thought the "perfect husband" did. Looking back, I should have asked her what her definition of the "perfect husband" was, and not assume.

Symptoms are things that people tell you. In the medical field, it could be something like, "My chest hurts," or "My knee hurts." We can't see the pain, but we can see the results of the pain. For example, if your child falls and hurts their knee, it hurts when he or she moves it, you can't see the pain itself, but you can see the expression of the pain on his or her face. The pain is a symptom and the facial expression is a sign. In a marriage, it is not easy to tell if something is a sign or a symptom. It is not important if it is a sign or a symptom. It is important to know that these are clues to something larger, and that you had better pay attention.

Let's explore some common signs and symptoms. If you see a sign or a symptom, you need to recognize it and start thinking. One sign or one symptom doesn't make you think something is happening. It should make you start thinking something is not right. When you see a set of signs, you should have bells going off in your head. Often in our marriages we ignore the signs and have a sense of denial. When you first see the dark clouds forming, you don't assume that things are going to be bad, but you start listening for thunder and looking for the lighting. One sign just causes us to stop and think. Now when you see lighting, hear thunder, and see the wind blowing, you know a storm is approaching. The same is true in a marriage.

There may be signs particular to your situation. You need to look for signs, but don't be a Sherlock Holmes and think everything is a sign. If you do, you will ruin the trust in your marriage, and it is hard to get back. Without trust, a marriage becomes a rocky road. You might just push your spouse to think about it harder. You are accusing him or her, so they might as well do it. It is hard to find the balance between trust and following the signs. You don't want to turn a blind eye to the situation, but you don't want to push your spouse over the edge either. Many people say that when they look back, they realize that they had a gut feeling that something was wrong, and that this gut feeling proved itself to be true. This may be the Holy Spirit telling us to pay attention to the signs and watch out for the next one. Most of the time you won't be able to see all the signs, until you look back. When you do, all the pieces will fall in to place. I feel that if we are going to stop divorce from killing our marriages. We need to know the signs, recognize what's about to take place, and <u>act</u>. If you felt like you were getting sick, wouldn't you schedule an appointment and go see the doctor?

People list the biggest cause of divorce is money problems. There are several different originations which teach financial management. Finical Peace University (Founded by Dave Ramsey) is very good. Crown Financial is also another wonderful program. I have taught both of them. They both share some of the same principals. I didn't know until I started teaching these courses how much people are in debt. Debt most defiantly puts a huge strain on the family. The good news is most people that go through one of these programs will work their way out of debt. The average time to be out of debt is 18 months. I have seen these programs work for many families. What would you do if you were out of debt? It is okay to dream here. The reality is that those dreams can come true. It just takes commitment and a little work.

Let's look at some more signs. Again, these are just some of what I have seen or been through. You may have different signs. Look for anything that pulls you apart or puts a barrier between you.

1. **You no longer have anything in common.** Of course, you will have children or family in common but when it is just you and your spouse, what do you talk about? What activities and interests do you share? If you don't have one, you need to develop one together. When you first met, you would talk on the phone for hours. You would look for things you had in common. You would search for things that you could enjoy together. You would plan time to do things together (dates). This helped to build common ground. As life happens, your focus shifts away from your spouse. You both work to support the family. Then children come along. You both push your own interests and your relationship to the back burner. We push this back to make room for work or kids. We get so involved with life that we don't take time to nourish our relationship with our spouse. My wife and I had only one daughter, and when she got married and started a life of her own, we looked at each other and both said, "Now what?" We had put so much time into raising our daughter and putting her through college that we left ourselves

somewhere along the road. In the beginning, we looked for things to help rebuild that common ground. We became a dull, lifeless, boring couple. I think this played a major factor in our divorce. If I took off work for a couple of days, or if we went on vacation, we would run out of things to talk about in about two days. We no longer shared common ground. When we were first married everything was new and exciting. Why couldn't we find new and exciting things after we had been married for years? It takes work and creativity to find new and exciting things to fill in some of these newfound cracks. Filling that void will help you return to a common ground. Studies have shown that lake of common interests allows other influences to hinder a strong relationship

2. **You can't do anything right.** Do you feel that no matter what you do, it is going to be done wrong? You can't do anything without your spouse making a snide remark or rolling their eyes. I am fascinated by nonverbal communication. Studies indicate that up to 80 percent of what we communicate is through nonverbal communication. It is not what you say with your mouth that people hear, but what you say through facial expressions and body language. Facial expressions, gestures, and eye movements are all forms of nonverbal

communication. Your mother was probably the best example of this. You know "the look" she gave you when she wanted to make you stop doing something irritating. You knew what would come next if you didn't stop what you were doing. Spouses do the same thing with each other, but they do it a little differently. For example, you do something that you think your spouse will like, but they turn up their nose or roll their eyes. Let's go back to what I thought was a "perfect husband": When my wife came home from work, I met her at the door. I would hug her and ask how her day was. Her normal response was to roll her eyes at me and not return the hug. After a few weeks of this, I stepped up my game. I would have a rose in my hand—nothing big, just something that came from our garden. I thought it would brighten her day and that I would get a different response. After all, it's the thought that counts, right? On these occasions, I would get an, "Oh thanks," and she would set it on the dresser on her way to the tub. That's where it would sit until I put it in some water. It didn't matter what I did: it was all wrong in my eyes. Everything was my fault, and I couldn't do anything right no matter how hard I tried. Negative criticism had worked its way into our relationship, and we were not able to overcome it. Hindsight—I should have asked what she needed.

3. **A change in appearance.** Does a change in appearance mean that something is wrong? No, but it can mean that a person is not happy with themself. Has your spouse started dying their hair or began wearing a different style of clothing, perhaps a younger style? Don't hear me say that trying to look younger is wrong or a bad thing, but it is a sign. Has your husband changed colognes? Has he or she started wearing a different style of underwear? Does he or she listen to different music? Or talk about buying a new sporty car? These are signs of a spouse who is unhappy with him or herself. This may mean that your husband or wife is looking for a change. It doesn't mean that an affair is imminent, but it is an indication of unhappiness or dissatisfaction. If these things are not discussed and the root problem is not dealt with, it could cause your spouse to look for a change outside your marriage. Now would be a good time to foster some common ground. Just think if you started exercising together or both of you updated your looks. Could this be some common ground? Sometimes people change their appearance because they feel that the marriage is threatened. Sometimes they change to try to keep everything together. A friend of mine thought her husband was having an affair. She began exercising and losing weight. She started dressing younger and dyed her hair a totally different color. She started to wear more

makeup. She did this to try and turn the head of her spouse. She was trying to hold on to him and change herself to what she thought he wanted.

A change in appearance is a sign that something is not right—it could mean that your spouse is not happy with him or herself, or that they feel the marriage is threatened. Either way, it is a red flag, and if nothing is done about it could lead to other things and the marriage will most likely suffer in one way or another. This could lead to the death of the marriage. Look for these as they may be subtle and hard to see until you are looking back.

4. **Withdrawal.** Withdrawal, or pulling away from each other, is very confusing for me. It can be as simple as not wanting to be near each other. There is a pulling away. This topic is very hard and confusing for me. It makes no sense at all.

Remember when you were first married? It was like you were attached at the hip. If you needed something from the store, you would turn off the game or your favorite TV show and go with your wife. This is where it starts to not make sense to me. This is what couples need the most: time together without distractions. The most valuable thing you have is your time. You choose what you do with it and with whom you spend it. It is something you will never get back.

The last few months of our marriage, we both knew that things were going south. We both knew that our marriage was in trouble. We took a few days off and planned a vacation—just us, so that we could work things out and try to put things together. We didn't go because of withdrawal. The pulling away had become too great and there was no willingness to try and put things back together. This withdrawal led us to suggest marriage counseling, which was the one thing, besides God that could have put us back together, the one thing that could have helped us the most. I still don't understand withdrawal and it still doesn't make sense to me. Recognize it, and head it off at the pass. Don't let it get inside your marriage. Stop it before it gets hold and causes you to do things that you don't want to do. The fact that the possible cure was close by and we didn't even try for it is very disheartening. Don't let this happen in your marriage.

5. **A change in habits.** If your spouse starts doing thing differently than they used to, this is a sign. People are creatures of habit. If you want to really study someone, look at their past. People don't deviate very much from patterns they have established. Habits take a strong

influence to change. Some say it takes twenty-one days to develop a new habit in your life. If your spouse starts spending more time at work or wants to go hang out with friends without you, this should be a red flag. If your spouse is hanging out with single friends, this is a big red flag. If she or he doesn't want you coming out on these outings, there is a reason. Men need playtime with male friends. Women also need time with friends. However, the influence these friends may have over your spouse is important. Playtime spent with the same sex is okay and can be helpful to the marriage, but there needs to be some rules. These go for both husband and wife. If your wife's playtime is spent at places where you would feel unwelcome, then this is a flag. If the playtime involves adult beverages, then this is a flag. It is healthy for husbands to have playtime with their buddies. It is also healthy for wives to have time with their friends. This will build a stronger marriage in the long run. Men need some time to talk about guy things and women need girl talk. It is imperative that there is a balance. If the man is the only one getting playtime, then it is detrimental to the marriage. Men, you can't go play cards at a buddy's house and not spend at least the same amount of time with your wife. You also need to let her have the same amount of time with her friends. There *has* to be balance.

The type activity is also important. If husbands go to establishments where women dance on tables, it will be detrimental to the marriage. If playtime is out of balance, the marriage is in jeopardy. On the other hand, if there is no playtime or time away from each other, this can also be a problem. After a while, you don't have anything to talk about. The marriage will seem stale or boring.

There must be rules, and if you have rules you must have consequences for breaking the rules. I am going to give you some rules that I think are important, but you and your spouse need to come up with your own rules. You also need to establish agreed-upon consequences for breaking the rules. You can always have more rules than suggested. Note: sex should never be withheld or used as a consequence. This will hurt the relationship in the long run.

Rule 1: Single people and married people should not go out together. If there is one or two people in the group that is okay. If your spouse is going off with a group of single people, then something is wrong. If you do this, you are asking for trouble. Single people and married people have different mind-sets and are looking for different things when they socialize. It only takes a wink or a little nod to start the mind on the path to temptation. Also the place that the group goes to is important and should be agreed upon before the playtime starts. The plan should be carried out. If something changes, then he or she needs to call his or her spouse and check in. If the spouse at home doesn't agree with the new plan, then his or her spouse needs to head home. For example: The guys decide to go out and play a round of golf. They get there and it turns out to be a closed tournament. So the guys change the plans and go to grab lunch. The place the group chooses is also the place the husbands' ex-girlfriend works. He needs to call his wife and check in. Not that he needs her approval, but if the shoe was on the other foot and it was his wife going out to eat. Things would be different. Remember, trust is a huge part of playtime.

Rule 2: Equal time for the spouse. If you get together and play poker on Monday nights, then you should spend Friday night with your wife. If there is no balance, it will cause resentment, and this will lead to bitterness. This will cause major problems in the marriage. Not only should husbands and wives spend as much time with each other as they do with their friends, but their playtime should also be equal. This cannot be one sided.

Rule 3: If you are fighting over playtime, it should be stopped. The value placed on a marriage needs to be at the top of the list *always*. If this is causing strife in the marriage, cease playtime for a while and reevaluate later.

Rule 4: Playtime should be over by bedtime. Crawling in bed alone is not fun. If your priorities come before your marriage, you will soon not have to worry about putting things before your marriage because there will be no marriage. Marriage must come first. Refer to rule # 3.

Rule 5: Playtime takes money. This money needs to be budgeted. This must be a strict rule and must be adhered to. If something comes up, and it takes your playtime money to cover it, guess what? No playtime. You can't take money away from the family to use for playtime. If you use money that is not allocated to playtime, this is a sign of addiction, and playtime needs to stop. Don't take money from your family just so you can have playtime. Both the husband and the wife need the same amount. If the husband likes to play golf and it cost around $ 50.00 to play. Then the wife needs the same amount to make things equal. Many times men will have the upper hand and this will not be equal. Remember this should be budgeted and planned out ahead of time. Spur of the moment activities can put a dent in a budget. If you don't have the extra money—WAIT!

In a perfect world, playtime would be a group of friends getting together with their families. They would spend time together cooking out or playing in the pool or something. The husband and wife would spend time together with the other couples and with the kids. Within this group, the men could get together and do something on their own, like playing cards or golfing. The women in the group could get together separately as well. Most of the time, the group should be together: husbands, and wives, and children. This is called community. This is what many churches strive toward. When you are a part of a community like this, it can be very positive for your marriage. These types of communities strengthen marriages and build strong families. This is the model for a successful marriage. A successful marriage is the key to a successful life. This also is a model for a successful church.

What happens most of the time is that Satan puts his smelly foot in the door and causes one of the marriages to have problems and end in divorce. The friends will take sides, or the group perceives that sides are drawn and the group falls apart. I've seen it happen way too often. This is the time that the group should rally around the couple and lift them up and help them through their troubles. Sadly, this is not what normally happens. Once the divorce takes place, the former couple won't fit in. The former couple will be left out of the planning of these gatherings. The new couples are rarely let back in the circle. New spouses or dates will feel like they are being compared to the former couple. They are never accepted fully to the circle. There are too many hurt feelings in the group.

6. **Intimacy:** This topic could have been included in the section on withdrawal, but it's so important that it deserved its own section. If this has taken a back burner in your marriage, your marriage is on a slippery slope and will crash hard. Lack of intimacy is often a sign that people notice but don't do anything about. If there is no intimacy in the marriage, the marriage is unlikely to last. The lack of intimacy plays a major role in couples that lead to divorce. Don't let me shock you; every marriage goes through a dry spell, but a dry spell that lingers is a warning sign. Intimacy is the glue that binds us together as husband and wife. If this is lacking in a marriage, it tells the spouse that there is no concern for the bond. Men need affection. It is in their fiber. A man's priorities are air, intimacy, and food—most of the time in that order. Try this at home: ask a man if he would rather eat or have sex. He will choose sex most of the time. He will eat a cold supper most every time. This is so important that Apostle Paul even wrote about it in his letter to the Corinthians.

1 Corinthians 7:1-5: "it is not good for a man not to touch a woman." He goes on to write in verse three, "Let the husband render to his wife the affection due to her, and likewise also the wife to her husband. The wife doesn't have authority over her own body, but the husband does. And likewise the husband doesn't have authority over his own body, but the wife does. Do not deprive one another except with consent for a time that you may give yourself to fasting and prayer; and come together again so that Satan does not tempt you because of your lack of self-control."

Intimacy builds the bond between a man and woman. In men, it builds self-control. Men and women will need this when they are confronted by temptation. It will help they control themself. It will not let their mind go to mush. In women, intimacy builds closeness and for some, self-esteem, which is something women struggle with. I don't know of a single woman that doesn't struggle with self-esteem. Some women struggle more than others. Women need to feel that closeness with their husbands—they need that bond. They need to know that he is going to be there for them. I think this goes way back in our history. History has shown, it was incredibly important for women to know that their husbands would be there to provide for them and their children. She needed to know that he would be there to protect her from animals or other men.

She even needs the bond to make her feel attractive. She needs to know that someone thinks she is pretty. She needs to know that she is desired. Most women need these feelings. They need to be made to feel secure. A woman needs to know that her man will be there for her and provide for her. I know what you're thinking: those things are different now, that times have changed. Women don't need men anymore to succeed. This is true, but I think that most women would choose to have a man around the house to help rather than remain single. I know you are probably thinking I still live under a rock. If you boil it all down, we need each other. If we don't have each other, then we have a huge hole in our heart and we try to fill it with a lot of things, most of which are unhealthy for us. Think about it for a few minutes.

I mentioned earlier that most marriages go through dry spells. Remember when you were first married. All you could think about during the day was your spouse. It was fun and exciting. We still need fun and excitement in our bedroom. There are many ways to keep it that way. Just don't force your spouse to do anything he or she doesn't think is right. Do not bring anyone else into the relationship. Even the thoughts of someone else will damage the relationship. The bible has some things to say about that sort of stuff and it will tell you it is wrong.

When you have kids, it makes this time a lot more difficult. This is why date nights are so important for a marriage. This should be budgeted for and scheduled. It shouldn't be done every week, but no more than a month should pass between dates. When you plan a date in advance, it builds excitement and anticipation. Dropping hints and leaving little messages helps make this fun and exciting. It doesn't have to be expensive or an overnight trip, but these dates are a must to building that bond that is vitally important in a marriage. Okay, here is my plug for grandparents: they love the kids as much, if not more, as they love you. When they call, who do they have to talk to before they hang up?

When they watch the grandkids, it helps to rekindle their nurturing instincts. It makes them feel younger. You grew up, and those feelings disappeared. Connecting with their grandchildren helps those feelings to reappear. If you don't have family close by, there is probably a couple in the church that would love to watch them for you. If nothing else, they would watch them to help you strengthen your marriage. I don't know of anyone who would turn down the opportunity to help you strengthen your marriage.

Intimacy is not just the act of sex. Men reread that last sentence. It is that loving touch on the side of the face, or that little pinch on the bottom. It could be getting out of your chair and cuddling on the couch. It's that soft caress that tells the other person that you love him or her that you are there for them. It tells him or her that he or she is desirable. It says that you're not going anywhere and that you want to be there with them. There are a lot of other places you could be but you choose to be there with them.

Marriages need a little spice; it's necessary to keep the marriage fun and exciting. Spice can take several different forms. Try and keep it reasonable: don't allow it to get out of hand. It can be something as simple as dropping a little note in your wife's lunch or left somewhere that only they will find it. Surprising your husband with a new nightgown will do wonders. Let your mind wander and have fun with it. Spend time thinking up the next new thing. Men, put some time and thought into it. Us men often plan on the fly and act like we have been planning all week. Women can see through this and will appreciate the effort that you put in.

One thing that works is putting five ideas on paper. Five for her and five for you. Don't let each other know what your five ideas are. Put them in separate bags and pull one out when it is your turn and prepare for it and do it on date night. It doesn't have to be complicated; it may be something simple. But if you open up and put some effort into it, it can be fun and exciting. It will be as fun as you make it. We men need to know what women want. We need help. We are not creative thinkers. That's just the way God made us. Try using one of the ideas for her and then let her do the next one for you. Once you start getting low on ideas, start the process over again. This will take some of the pressure off the guys, and the women will get something that they want. Men, don't make this only a sexual thing. She may want a bubble bath and foot rub. Be open to making her happy. This is just one way to open the lines of communication. Ok this is a shameless plug, go to stopping-divorce.com to share and find ideas.

Communication is very important in intimacy. Respect each other's feelings. Things like this keep the relationship from becoming stale and boring. The definition of insanity is doing the same thing over and over, and expecting different results. I worked with a guy, and his thought on marriage and relationships was, "Why do I want to eat only vanilla ice cream for the rest of my life, when I can have different ice cream flavor whenever I want?" My answer to his theory was vanilla is what God wants us to have; it is the way he planned it. Vanilla with a few cookies or nuts every now and then to spice it up will taste a lot better in the long run than switching to other flavors.

Don't go to an extreme. Don't do anything that will cause your mother to go, "Eww." Stay within reason, and, like I said earlier, don't allow any outsiders. Pornography is a trap made by the devil. Pornography will cause you to start comparing yourself or your mate to something that is not real. It will cause you to do things that your spouse may not want to do. Sometimes they will do them and compromise to just to make you happy. They don't enjoy them but it is what you want. Be mindful of the others feelings. Don't put pressure on your spouse to do something that will cause hurt feelings or make him or her feel dirty.

While doing research for this book I came across a topic called HSDD that is not widely known; many doctors don't even know about it. HSDD stands for Hypoactive Sexual Desire Disorder (low sexual desire). From what I can understand, HSDD is a disorder that is a physical problem that causes decreased sexual desire. This can occur for several reasons. Many of them are treatable and can be very easy to control. The main problem is that HSDD often goes untreated, or women are told that it is all in their head. Most often doctors will tell the patients to go home and drink some wine and relax. This doesn't seem to be the right treatment, and it causes women to feel inadequate. Men will often internalize HSDD and think that it is their fault also. This is a new field of study and doctors will hopefully develop a treatment that many couples need. This is a real problem and they are just now beginning to understand it. Research it, and seek the right doctors if you think this is a problem in your marriage. Have patience and don't give up until you get the results you need.

These are just a few signs or symptoms. There are many more. You will have signs that are unique to your situation. I think if you boil it all down, it comes to a gut feeling. Most of the time your gut feeling will lead you in the right direction. If you have a gut feeling, many times it is true. Your gut will clue you in to something fishy going on. Don't hesitate to talk to your spouse about your gut feelings. You will need to work through them. You will need to confront your spouse who has these feelings. Remove their doubt by being transparent. Show them you have nothing to hide. Look for signs that your spouse is not telling the truth. Most spouses will become defensive and will try and defend his or her position. If your spouse does this, it should raise another flag, as it indicates that he or she may be hiding something. Sometimes this will cause your spouse to think about his or her behavior and stop it, or he or she may try and hide it even more.

If your spouse confronts you with a suspicion of wrongdoing, it is time to change your behavior if you're doing something wrong. If you are not doing anything wrong, be open and try everything possible to allay your spouse's fears. If this means no playtime or more time around the house, then do it. Your whole goal in life is to make your spouse feel comfortable and loved.

A friend of mine came to me one day and told me he was having marital problems. He told me that his wife thought he was having an affair and he honestly wasn't. I told him that he needed to do everything to make her believe that he wasn't having an affair. During our discussion, I told him, "If she wants you to wear a chicken suit and hold a sign on a busy street that says "I love my wife," would you do it?" Of course that is a silly example, but it shows your spouse that you are willing to do anything possible to make the marriage work. Will you do what it takes to make it work?

God gave us a spouse as a helper, and for security. A spouse is a gift from God. Do you think that the person that fell in love with you did it just to have something to do? No! God placed that person in your life. Do you think God would give you something and then take it back? Don't you think that God would give you a perfect gift? Are you honoring God's gift to you? Don't you know what your children need even before they ask for it? Are we not God's children? Don't you think God knows what we need even before we ask?

How are you treating God's gift? Are you treating it like a dog that lives under the porch? Sometimes you call out and play with it. Sometimes it gets in the doorway and protects you. Sometimes we don't want to be bothered with it and chase it off the porch because we don't want to spend time with it. Sometimes it stinks badly. Sometimes we take care of it and wash it and nurture it and love it. Sometimes we chase it away and don't let it come back home. Don't treat God's gift like this. Your marriage is something beautiful and of great value. Your marriage is something to be honored. If it not functioning like it should, then fix it. It is the greatest relationship outside of your relationship with God. Do everything in your power to make it what you want it to be. God will be there to help you through it and help you make it through the tough times. He will also be there in the good times, celebrating with you. He is not going to let you go through something alone. He will help you nurse your marriage back to health.

Hebrews 13:4–5. "Marriage is honorable among all, and the bed undefiled; but fornicators and adulterers God will judge. Let your conduct be without covetousness; be content with such things as you have. For he himself has said, 'I will never leave you or forsake you.'"

This passage says that if we are adulterers that God will judge us. We need to be content with the gift that God has given us without looking for something new and improved. We should be content. His promise is, "He will never leave us or forsake us." God is going to be there for us and help us through whatever mess we cause.

1 Peter 3:7. "Husbands, likewise dwell with them [wives] with understanding, giving honor to the wife, as to the weaker vessel, and as being heirs together of the grace of life, that your prayers may not be hindered."

We need to honor our wives and live with them with understanding. We are not built like them, and we certainly don't think like them. Women don't think like men and can't do the things that men can do. We are different. We have different roles in life. That's why God put us together. Two people working together can accomplish more than one person working alone. The things that I don't do well are her strengths. The things she doesn't do well are my strengths. Together we work like a well-oiled machine. We are together in this thing called life. We are together to show each other grace. If we honor our spouses, then our prayers will not be hindered. If two people start working against each other, will any work getting done? Honor your spouses. They are there for a reason. They are there to help you.

We started this chapter talking about signs and symptoms to watch out for. We also talked about ways to correct the signs as we recognize them. The important thing is to watch out for signs and recognize that we need to change our behavior. Prevention is always the best way to handle a problem. I asked a lot of questions. Hopefully you will take time to look back over some questions that I raised. I hope it causes you to think. Now is time for a little reflection. Think back over the signs that we discussed. Are you noticing any signs? Is your spouse noticing any of these signs in you? If you said "yes" or "maybe," put this book down and go talk to your spouse. Get these things worked out. There is no better time than the present to start the communication process. Before you talk to your spouse, take a minute and ask God to help you through this important situation. Spend some time in prayer.

God will be there to help you.

Effects of the Disease

I think that most people who go through a divorce don't understand the realities that follow it. They don't understand the feelings that come crashing down on them after the divorce is final. I don't think they consider how the divorce will affect the children. I think that if they had a crystal ball and could look in to the future and see the pain and sorrow that occurs after the divorce, they would think twice about continuing with the divorce. I feel that most people would not go through with it. Most people think in the short-term. They think, "Oh, you have hurt me, so I'm going to hurt you." Or they think, "I have been wronged and I can't take it anymore." Most people don't take realize that the divorce will affect the children for the rest of their lives. Just because you are angry and feel like you can't take it anymore, it doesn't justify divorce. God promises that he will never allow pressure to come upon you greater than what you can bear. He will never leave you or forsake you.

There are four groups of people that are affected in divorce. We will look at these groups and try to glimpse the emotions and feelings that each group will go through. However, different people will have different feelings, and each situation is different. These are a combination of feelings that I went through and also that others have been through. I think the emotions are very similar in each situation. Most people don't think about these feelings prior to the divorce. I hope this is a glimpse of what is on the other side of the fence; it might not look like you expect. You have heard the saying that the grass always looks greener on the other side of the fence. Let's look at the grass closely. My hope is that in looking at the grass, you may decide to stay on your side of the fence and nurture it.

The four groups of people that are affected are:

1. The divorcee: this is the person who wants the divorce. This is the person that thinks the grass is greener on the other side. The court calls this person the plaintiff.

2. The divorced: this is the person who is divorced. This is the person that gets left with the shambles of what used to be a family. The court calls this person the defendant.

3. The friends and the family of the divorced couple.

4. The children, who will be affected for the rest of their lives

Let's look at each group and see how they are affected.

1. **The divorcee**. This person has grassy eyes. They feel like they have been wronged. They feel like they can't take it anymore. This person is a quitter. Yes, I said a quitter. They don't want to fight for the marriage; they don't want to do what it takes to save it. All they want to do is run away. Even though they think they have the backbone to stand up for themself, they are spineless. They have given up. They think it is time to cross the fence and move on to greener pastures. Those pastures have the same smell and taste as the pasture they are in; it just takes time to realize it. They don't want to look and see that the grass is the same with the same rocks and boulders in it. The pasture looks different, but it still has rocks and boulders. These people have visions of grandeur. They think that life will be different if they only: fill in the blank. People are basically the same. We all work, sleep, and eat. We all brush our teeth. How can this be different than what they had at home? You might get an answer like, "The other person treats me better. "Yes, this may be true for a while, but sooner or later it will feel the same. I am not talking about abusive

situations. *No one* should live in an abusive situation. *No one* should lay a hand on you or your children in anger. If this happens, get out as fast as you can. Most marriages in the United States end because of money problems or infidelity. Once you cross the fence, the money may be different, but if it is managed the same way as before, it will soon become the same as before. Sooner or later, the new person will become just like the one you left. If you leave because of an affair, look out. If a person divorces once, they will do it again. According to Divorcecare Ministries most second marriages have a 70 percent failure rate.

Let's talk about the feelings the divorcee will experience. They will soon feel like the bad person in the marriage. First, they will feel alone and insecure about the decision and will feel abandoned. They will feel like none of the family or friends approve of them anymore. They will feel left out of a lot of things: They will grow lonely. They will feel that there is a lot of hatred toward them for breaking up the marriage. I think there will be a point in time when they say to themself, "I've really screwed up this time, and I've lost most of my friends and family that cared for me." Or, "I really caused a big mess this time." Some people will wallow in this self-pity for a long time. They made the choice to run away; they just didn't know what they were running to. They feel like the kids hate them and will often try to buy their love. We all know this is not the best for the kids. It makes them materialistic and money hungry.

In my opinion, God looks down on these people and is sad. He could have saved the marriage if they would have only trusted in him. The divorcee will live in a dark lonely place and will seek approval from many places and not feel satisfied from within.

2. **The divorced**. This is me. I can tell you from experience what this feels like. I want to explain this side because most of the divorcees don't get the chance to see this side because those that are unfaithful are skipping along or curled up in someone else's arms without a thought of the pain the divorced person is going through. It's like they don't want to see it, or they want us to go through this pain as punishment.

The divorced feels . . . I don't really know how to put it in words. I don't know where to start. A lot of these emotions are all mixed up inside. I am like most men and am level-headed and don't show emotions very well. Most men are taught to not show emotions. So, I put on a happy face and went out into the world without letting people see that I was a train wreck on the inside. I didn't let people see what went on behind closed doors.

I am the type of person that people can count on in a crisis. My profession is one that takes a very chaotic problem and brings order. My job is to make things better. I couldn't do that in my private life; I didn't know how to make it better. I couldn't fix it. I spent many nights balled up on the floor, crying like a baby and angry at God. I cried out to him, "Why?" and asked him to take the pain away. I felt like I had caused my own pain and that I had somehow pushed my wife away. I know now that this was not true and probably felt that it wasn't true then, but I had no other explanation as to why I felt so much pain. It was a physical pain, and it even hurt to breathe at times. I felt like something was wrong with me. I felt like I was an ugly, horrible monster who didn't know how to treat people. I felt like no one else could love me because I was so terrible. I didn't know if I was capable of treating a person the way they deserved to be treated.

It was a long, horrible road to go down.

When morning came, it was time to put on the happy face and walk out the door into the world. It was very hard to work like this. I would often go into the bathroom and cry. I would then have to give myself a pep talk just to walk out of the bathroom. In the Bible, Paul tells us "to pray continuously."**(1 Thessalonians 5:17)** I know what that feels like. My every thought was consumed with the pain and uncertainty I was facing.

Work ended and I had to go home, but home was no longer a welcoming place. It was dark and lonely. Sometimes I would go shopping and walk around just so I didn't have to walk back in to that dark, lonely house. I walked in the house and was constantly reminded of my wife. I saw her all over the house and was reminded of all the good and bad. You see things that you helped her pick out. For example: we drove over a hundred miles to pick out our living room set. My mother-in-law went with us. We ate at a very good country restaurant and went to a yard sale before driving home. We came home a different way, and my wife started to get sick on the curvy roads. Even how we arranged the furniture brought back memories. I helped her hang the pictures. We designed the house to our own plans. Even the bed in the bedroom was significant: we spent several months looking for just the right one. When you look around the house, you see pictures of the kids. I'm sure some of these feelings are similar to feelings of grief when you lose a loved one.

As you sit and think about all these memories, the thought of your spouse with someone else creeps into your head.

You imagine them curled up on the couch watching the same TV show you used to watch together. *What a feeling.* The divorcee doesn't have to look at all these things every day, day in and day out. It doesn't seem fair.

I can remember working on Christmas Eve and having to come home on Christmas day to a dark, lonely house. It was the loneliest I have ever felt. It was a very tough time for me. Yes, Christmas time is a time of family and joy, a time of celebration. I think I would have rather taken a beating than open that door and walk into the cold, dark, lonely, place that morning. The quiet place that had become my home. Just thinking of it still brings tears to my eyes. I came in and put my bag down and hit the floor crying. I called out to God, "Why?" I felt like a terrible monster that no one loved. I knew that my daughter and parents loved me, but it wasn't the same. I felt like Frankenstein. After a few days, I became consumed with anger and bitterness. I was mad at her for putting me through this pain. It got to such a point that I became physically ill. Not only was I unable to sleep, but I developed ulcers. I was mentally, physically, and spiritually a wreck.

I can't leave you there. I am a problem-solver like most men. I knew what I needed to do, but I just couldn't do it. Even though I had often wanted to drive to her house and pull what's-his-name out of the house and beat him unconscious, this was not what I needed to do. I knew I had to forgive her. This was very hard, but I had to do it for my health and sanity. I locked myself in the house without my phone or TV. I spent so much time on my knees that my knees and shoulders hurt for several days, but I had to get on my knees before God.

Finally, I came to a place of forgiveness, but it was a long battle. I had to let go and allow God to take control. I gave it all to God. Of course I ran to him and took it back several times, but I ended up giving it to him fully. It was like the world had been lifted off me, and I could finally breathe again. I could have a thought on my own, and it wasn't about her. I was a new person: no more happy face. It was truly a life-changing experience. Those feelings of grief and self-pity still come every now and then, but I am able to work through them. They still sneak up on me and jump on me when I'm not looking, but those days get farther and farther apart. I know that God is in control, and if he has truly shut the door to my marriage of thirty years, then he has a new door for me to go through when I'm ready.

3. **Friends and family**. Most of the friends and family members don't know what to say. They stand off at a

distance. They don't want you to feel like they have taken sides, and they don't want you to feel like they are meddling. They do want to know what happened because they care about you. The friends will be divided. They may not take the side you expect. The family will be supportive to a point. They will try to stay in touch and invite you over for special occasions. You will find yourself asking if they are asking because they care, or if they're asking out of a sense of duty. They may be looking for a Jerry Springer moment. We don't always understand the intentions of others. Your family should be there for you, but they too will be standoffish. The divorcee might even feel that the family has abandoned him or her. They may feel like the family has taken the other side. This is a horrible feeling, but it is what it is. They may not know the full story, and every story has at least two sides. Both of these sides will be told with a slant. I am not suggesting that you broadcast the whole story at Thanksgiving, but not everyone may know all the details. People will believe their own versions, no matter what they are.

Friends have a tough job. They want to stay friends with both people, but in the long run this may not happen: sooner or later they will take sides. Or perhaps they will not take sides and distance themselves from both parties.

They will become acquaintances. This is sad because both parties need good strong friends to be there for them. You need someone you can call on those days when everything seems bad. You need someone that will be there and tell you when you're being stupid.

When I was growing up, my family was very close to my cousin's family. My cousin was close to my age. We did a lot together growing up. When we reached dating age, we dated a couple of girls that were close friends. I got married to one, and he married the other. This was great. We did a lot of things together after we were married. We would go on vacations together. We would spend many weekends' together playing cards. Our kids were friends. Everything was going great. They started to have marital trouble. They caught the virus and their marriage died as a result. This started to cause problems in our marriage. My wife and I took sides, whether we wanted to or not. We had to come to an agreement in our marriage that we were going to hold firm and not let their divorce interfere with our marriage. We vowed not to let their problems become our problems. Their marriage died and our marriage suffered because we wanted to be there for them but we both couldn't be there for the both of them. Don't be surprised if you lose friends, even close friends. Expect them to pull away for a time and then choose sides. It just happens. You might not want it to happen, but it happens most of the time. This is very sad because you need friends most at this time.

4. **The Children**. This is the group that takes the divorce very hard. The poor children experience a life-changing event that they had nothing to do with. Many of them are completely isolated from what's going on they are often shunned from the problem until things are decided for them. Most people don't want to fight in front of the children. The children still know something is not right and that mommy and daddy's relationship is strained. While it is not their fault, many children blame themselves for their parents' divorce. The age of the child has a great bearing on how the child reacts. Overall, most children want mommy and daddy to get back together and be a happy family again. Children don't get to see everything that goes on, and all they can remember are the good times the family had together. If they do see their parents fight, it reinforces the idea that they are somehow the cause of the fight. They feel they are to blame. These two feelings are the same no matter the age of the child. My daughter was married and had a child when this happened in our household. She still had these feelings—she won't admit it, but they were there. The children are put in a difficult place in the

relationship. They are forced to take sides. They know one of the parents is to blame.

Let's look at the different age groups and how they are affected. Since I don't hold any degree other that the degree of hard knocks, the information I present to you has been gathered from DivorceCare classes and e-mails. DivorceCare is an excellent ministry. They present a biblical view of divorce and the emotions that it brings to the surface. They helped me to understand what was going on in my head and heart. The classes gave me a biblical perspective as to what was going on in my own life.

Infants and toddlers: They can tell that something is not right. They are often taken out of their routines. They may be live in a different place. They tend to have more infections and illnesses. This is just what the custodial parent needs: a child who is fussy. This just increases stress levels.

Preschool: Many preschool-aged children don't understand what's going on and may wonder where the other parent is, and they may ask for the other parent repeatedly. This will cause separation anxiety and they will become clingy. They often regress in their behavior. They need to be reassured that the parent will be there for them.

Ages 5–8: This is a tough age for children anyway. This is the time they are going to school and having to deal with all the emotions that come along with that. If a parent is then missing during this time, it puts an extra burden on the child's parent. Suddenly that parent has to get the child off to school and check homework all on his or her own. Many times the children's grades will suffer, and they will begin to act out at school. They may have a non-caring attitude. Some feel this is due to the feelings that the other parent doesn't care about them. They need more adult time, and they need to know that both parents care. They feel left out and need reassurance. They need to know that you will be there for them. They need both parents.

Age 9–12: This age group is trying to define themselves. They are trying to figure out who they are. They will be developing their own self-esteem. They are starting to place value on themselves. They are also old enough to start placing blame. Often times, they will blame themselves. This age group needs the parents to get back together. They dream that the parents will get back together, and they often concoct plans to reunite their parents. Often times this will involve them acting out so the parents will be forced to talk to each other. Sometimes this will involve fights with the custodial parent and will involve them wanting to go live with the other spouse. This age group takes divorce very hard.

Teenagers: This age group will handle the divorce differently than others. They might be angry or depressed or act out: each teenager will handle it differently, even teenagers in the same family. They have and feel the hurt, but they lack the ability to put it in words. It is like being kicked in the stomach and not being able to tell anyone how it hurts. My heart goes out to this age group. I have worked with them. The children of divorced parents are constantly seeking approval, and they seek it most from their peers or members of the opposite sex. They will often do things to be noticed; many of them will do anything to be accepted. Their self-esteem is at rock bottom. They just want to fit in and feel normal. Boys in this group will try and be the clown or they will play the outcast and wear clothes and hairstyles that are unpopular. Girls will wear lots of makeup or dress provocatively. They may act provocatively in order to attract the attention of the opposite sex. They take divorce very hard. Teen pregnancy is high among this group. They are looking for love, the love of the missing parent. They are not getting enough of it at home. Girls *need* their daddies. Girls need the approval of their daddies. Don't take my word for it—analyze other families that have divorced parents. Look at the behavior of the children. Talk to youth leaders in churches. Volunteer or chaperone with this age group. It will become very evident which children come from broken homes. If the parent is on the third, fourth, or even fifth marriage, the children's behavior will be even more pronounced. They feel all alone, and they need to know that you care about them. They need to know that you love them. They also need discipline. To them, discipline means love. They won't be able to tell you this and will often rebel from discipline. As they get older and look back, they will know that you cared. This may not be evident to them now, but they will one day look back and know the truth. Hopefully it will not be too late.

I don't mean to scare you . . . okay, yes; I do want to scare you. If you are thinking about divorce and haven't looked at the other side of the fence clearly, you need to be scared. Many people look over the fence, but they see through rose-colored glasses. They don't see the full picture. Their vision is skewed. There are many consequences of divorce. Not only is the divorcing couple affected, but the family and friends are affected as well. Most people don't take this into account when they are thinking about divorce. They don't think about the effects on the children or their friends. I hope this section forces you to think before you leap over the fence. I hope you think about others and how your actions affect them and take that into account before you make that decision. I hope that if you have looked over the fence, this section will help you to see more clearly. I hope this gives you a little more strength to climb back down off the fence and do whatever it takes to make *your* side of the fence look better. Grass looks better when it is nurtured and fertilized and watered. Who says your grass can't be the best yard around? Who says that your yard can't be brought back to health? With the right care, your yard *can* be the best yard around. You can water and fertilize it and make it stronger. Stronger than it has ever been. Your yard can be the yard that everyone tries to emulate. It takes time and hard work to make it look beautiful. It can get there, but it takes three: you, your spouse, and a relationship with the maker of the universe.

With prayer, *all* things are possible.

Treatments

There are times in a marriage when either spouse feels badly treated. People feel angry and bitter when their expectations are unmet. People have this grand idea of how their life should be, but this may or may not be what God has planned for them. Men and women have different ideas of what life should look like. Many women want white picket fences and 2.3 kids. This is what society tells us that we need to be normal. Society tells us that men want sexy supermodels for wives. Is this true? Is this what we really want? I have talked to several women and I work with mostly men. I don't think this is what we want. We will take the next few minutes to explore what I have put together. No, I don't have a PhD or a background in psychology; I am just a plain old Joe commissioned by God to help relieve the pain of divorce that is running throughout our nation. We need to re-formulate what is normal. Do our ideas of what it means to be normal come from television? Normal is just like your body temperature: it can be different for different people. My normal body temperature is 97.8. I like to watch student nurses when they take my temperature. The look on their face is priceless. The national normal temperature is 98.6. The textbook normal for blood pressure is 120/80. However, the textbooks give you a range. And as long as the blood pressure is within that range, it is not a concern. The Bible gives us guidelines for how to behave. It also gives us boundaries for marriage. We need to focus on these guidelines and not what the world thinks is normal. Most certainly we should not be guided by what we see on TV. Sometimes our parents don't model a good example for us, either. However, this doesn't mean that we can't model a good, wholesome God-fearing marriage before our children.

What Do Men Want in a Marriage?

Let's look at what men want. I know I will get off track here, but bear with me—everything will come together in the end. Men are just little boys. Most men don't mature beyond age thirteen. Let's look at the thirteen-year-old boy. He is old enough to do most things by himself. He will do most things he is made to do. But where is his mind? It is in the backyard playing with his friends. He is thinking about playing and cutting up. He is looking for his next adventure, whether it is slaying dragons in the backyard or hunting for buried treasure. When he is with his friends, the whole world stops and he is living out his life as someone else. He has to be made to come in and do his homework.

Let's compare the thirteen-year-old boy to the adult man. Most men can do things on their own, whether it is running a business or doing a job. Men know that they have to provide for their family. They will do what they need to do to make this happen. Does that mean that men will like it? No, but they will do what is necessary. Men need goals and objectives. We need to know what to do at specific times (we will come back to this). When men get together with their friends, what happens? They will joke around and sooner or later there will be burping and scratching and if they are comfortable with each other, farting. Men will joke and cut up all night if you let them. Most of the time their real name will not be used. Nicknames will be the order. Sparky, Super Cooper, and old man just to name a few.

What men need in marriage is a playmate, but not the Hugh Heffner type. They need a best friend. They need someone they can cut up with on a regular basis. They need someone they can share adventures with. It may not be slaying dragons in the backyard, but it may be a sport. The wife needs to be this playmate. Male bonding is very important and is needed. However the husband and wife need this play time together also. Consider taking up a sport together or a hobby. This will bring the couple closer than anything. Women seem to have a hard time hanging out in this manner they prefer more structure. Would you want your husband to hang out with you or some of his college buddies?

Let's camp out here for a moment.

Men need to know that they are accepted by their wives, no matter what. Let's talk about something that happens far too often and has a chance to destroy a marriage. Some women feel like they need to be in charge. I don't know if it is that marriage is not enough for them, or if they feel like things are stale and boring. But for some reason they begin to belittle their man. The big word for this is emasculate. Men are like dogs. You throw a ball and the dog brings it back to you. You praise the dog. What happens the next time you throw the ball? The dog brings it back. Now, on the other hand, if you scold the dog with a negative tone when he retrieves the ball, what happens? The dog will sometimes bring the ball back in hopes of being praised for doing it right. But if he is scolded for doing what he thought was right, how long will he continue to return the ball? From then on, if you pick up the ball what happens? The dog will roll his eyes and walk the other way, fearing that no matter what he does it will not be right and that he will sooner or later get scolded.

Women often punish men without even knowing it. For example, a woman may say, "This trash fills up quickly." This is woman-speak for, "Get up right now and take out the trash." Men, however, hear only that they make a lot of trash. The next comment she might make is, "Somebody needs to take out the trash." What the husband hears is, "One of the kids needs to take out the trash." He may think, "Okay, I'll get it when a commercial comes on and do it." The next thing he hears is, "I guess I'll have to take out the trash." The man now gets up from watching TV and takes the trash out. When he returns from taking out the trash, his wife is visibly angry. She starts fussing about how he never helps her around the house and how lazy he is. The next time the trash gets close to the top, the husband takes it out ahead of time without being told. He waits for his wife to compliment him for being so proactive. He even hints about it, but she never says anything. He tells her he took out the trash. What is her response? "Yes, you did, but you didn't help with the dishes, and you didn't pick up the clothes." This is just like hitting the dog after he brings the ball back.

Men need positive reinforcement. We need to know that we are doing something good. If not, what we think is, "Why carry out the trash? She will still fuss about it or she will find something else to fuss about, so why bother? I might as well give her something to complain about, since she will do it anyway." Not those men are golden retrievers and need to be praised about every little thing. If this carries on for several years, then soon the wife starts to believe that her husband is useless and worthless and never helps around the house. This emasculates him in her eyes. She starts to believe that he is no longer the one for her. She starts thinking about the grass being greener on the other side. If she treats him like he can't do anything right, sooner or later nothing he does will be good enough in her eyes. I'm not going to point fingers and say she created this mess, but I have seen it happen to me and several of my friends. I don't share this with you to ask for your pity, but as an example of the things I did to try and overcome the stigma of not being able to do things right.

This is an example of when I was doing everything I knew how to do and as I look back it emasculated me. We had talked about how she wanted to leave the marriage. She would come home from work, and I would have her bubble bath ready. Along with the bath, I would have something for her to drink while in the tub. Sometimes it was a glass of wine. I would also have some chocolate waiting for her. I would sit next to the tub and talk to her about her day. This was her time to share her day with me. Halfway through the bath, I would leave her alone to relax and finish cooking supper. She would get out of the tub and supper would be ready. We would eat supper and I would put away the dishes. She would check her e-mail or play a game on the computer. We would then watch TV. She would fall asleep on the couch. I would then turn back the bed and put her into it. She worked about an hour away, so she had to get up early. This wasn't just something I did on special occasions—it was our routine every night I was home. I was trying to be good enough. I was emasculated and felt that I could do nothing right. As I look back, I feel like an idiot for jumping through those hoops. However, at the time I was trying to save a marriage. I would have stood on the street in a chicken suit and sung the star spangled banner if it would have made a difference.

Men need

1. A playmate: someone to joke and cut up with, someone to share their life with. This should be their spouse.

2. Men need to be told they are doing a good job. They work better with positive reinforcement than with scolding.

3. Men need someone who cares about them no matter what.

4. Men need to know that even though the world outside is a tough place to live. That when he gets home he will be welcomed with open arms.

Men need a safe, comfortable place to fall when the world is crazy, when things are getting out of hand. Men need a fort to come to and feel safe. Men need to know that when the economy is bad and jobs are being cut and the boss is cranky, they can come home to a wife who will stand by them no matter what happens. At the end of the day, he can curl up in her arms and feel loved. Men need to feel like knights in shining armor. Even though the world is crazy, once he steps inside the door of his fort, he is the defender and the hero. Watch little boys when they play. They act out that they are the guy that kicks the bad guy's butt. They are rock stars, or they hit the homerun and scored in the bottom of the ninth inning, with the bases loaded. Men just want to be the hero, if only in his wife's eyes. Remember we are only thirteen on the inside.

When a pretty woman talks to a thirteen-year-old boy, he becomes shy and is somewhat embarrassed. When he gets back to his friends, they tell him they can't believe she was talking to him. "I think she likes you," they tell him. His friends are secretly saying to themselves, "I wish she would talk to me." Men need this same feeling about their wives. Not that they need a supermodel all the time, but when they are out at special gatherings (work parties, weddings, etc.) they need their buddies to be thinking, "Wow." Not that women need to look this way all the time, but it makes a man feel good to know that everyone in the room is looking at his wife. Inside he is thinking, "Yes, she is pretty, but she is actually going home with me. Wow, I am a somebody?" I am not saying anorexia and plastic surgery is the way to go. A dirty tank top and sweat pants are okay, around the house but for going to the grocery store. Looking attractive will go a long way to keeping your man's eyes on you.

What Do Women Want?

I will have to be very honest here: I don't know what women want. I have tried to understand what they want, and have done research and looked up studies. I have come to the conclusion that I am not qualified to say what women want. For the men reading this book, put it down and go ask the significant women in your life what women want. Ask friends and mothers. But first ask your wife. This will open up lines of communication and show your wife that you truly want to make her happy. I have heard all the jokes surrounding this subject; I will refrain from including any here. I think this topic is the reason I began writing this book. I didn't know what my wife wanted, and I was wrong about what I thought she wanted. At the time I didn't think I could do anything right. My attempt to process the events that took place around my divorce spurred this book along with God's guidance.

When it comes to showing your wife that you love her, I have found that there are at least two types of women. The two categories of women have different views on how we love them. If you don't know how she feels loved, then you will certainty have trouble down the road? Let me explain the two types and it will clear some of this up for you.

Category 1: The woman that likes flowers, gifts, and notes. This is how she feels loved.

Category 2: The woman that feels loved when you help around the house: cooking supper, cleaning. She feels loved when you help without being told.

Most women will fall into one of these categories. Of course all women like getting gifts, and most women will appreciate help around the house. However, the way that they feel most loved will be fall into one of these categories. Take a category two woman who feels loved when someone cooks or cleans the house for her. If you shower her with gifts and flowers, she will like them, but she won't feel as loved as she would have if you had done the laundry or had fixed a meal. On the other hand, if you have a category one woman, and you take the kids for the evening or wash her car, she isn't going to feel that special love that she would have if you had brought her flowers. Things can change throughout the marriage. If you do special things often this may become normal and expected. It is worth trying both approaches occasionally—mix things up. Men become creatures of habit. We think that we can do the same thing over and over again and get the same results. When it comes to women, this is not always the case. Seek out what she likes, but and don't do it every day. Space things out, but not too far. I think we, as men, get caught up in life and don't think about doing things for our spouse. We don't realize we need to do more gestures until we are in trouble or we think something is not right at home. Certainly don't make these loving gestures insincerely, or because you have done something wrong or are in the doghouse. Hint: if you do these things only to get out of the doghouse, you will find yourself there more often. Sometimes it is that she wants more, or she knows that you do this when you have been bad and will wonder if she has something to worry about. Do these gestures just because you want her to know that you love her.

Like I have confessed, I don't know what women want, so I called in reinforcements. I asked a few of the women that God has put in my life. Some of these women were only there for a short period of time. I believe that God put them there to help me through this topic. I asked them what they wanted in a marriage. As you will find, the women's answers have a common thread that runs through all of them. I hold all of these women in high regard and respect them a great deal. They all have different backgrounds and different perspectives. I have included a small portion of their background to help you understand each perspective. It is interesting that even though their lives are so different, they often want similar things.

The first is Teresa. She is a wonderful friend and has helped me through the past few years of divorce silliness. She is a wonderful mother and wife, and I am honored to call her my friend. She grew up in a small town and married her high school sweetheart. She stuck by his side all through college. When her husband entered the work force, she stayed at home and raised the children. Her husband has risen to the top of his career and has a high-pressure, high-paying job. This has caused them to move all over the country. That alone will put a strain on a marriage. They have been married for over thirty-five years and are still in love. Their children have lives of their own now. When I asked Teresa what she wants in a marriage, she told me that she wants complete honesty. Because of her husband traveling a lot, this is imperative. Excitement and a best friend also rank high on her list. She wants someone with whom she can share *everything*. She wants someone to honor, love, and cherish her, someone who is in it for the long haul. She says that she needs someone to share things with, both good and bad times.

The next is Lynn. She is a wonderful lady who has endured a lot in her life. She was married for thirty years, and her husband was unfaithful to her for most of their marriage. In an effort to keep harmony in her family, she endured the affairs. When she caught him with a girl younger than their daughters, she'd had enough. She took a stand and divorced him. This was new life for her, and standing alone against the world was very scary. When I asked her what she wanted in a marriage, her word was commitment. This has a wide meaning to her. It means commitment to family, the marriage, the spouse, and to financial solvency. This is a strong word for her. Commitment to her means being there, in both body and mind. To Lynn, commitment means forsaking *all* others, like it is stated in the Bible. It is a commitment to the spouse no matter what may come up. It means spending time with her and being attuned to her and her needs and desires. It means being financially sound and not hiding money from the family.

My friend Tori has had some horrible things happen in her life. Despite these negative experiences, she has a heart the size of Texas and loves doing things for others. She has no struggle with money. She has been through things that most people only hear about. She has been through the molestation of a child by someone close to the family. She has endured the deaths of close friends. She is a very loving woman, but she has very high emotional walls. If you try and get close to her, she will throw you back over the wall. She is a new Christian and has the heart of an evangelist. She wants to tell everyone about her God. When I ask her what she wants in a marriage, she responded that she wants honesty and acceptance. She wants someone to share life with, the joys and the burdens. She wants integrity. She wants a role model for her children. She wants someone who can lead, someone who can be the head of the household, who can take control and give direction to the family and the marriage. She wants someone who can lead her and her family by following Christ. Her past has forced her to be both mother and father to her children. She would like to return to being their mother. She wants someone to hold her when things go wrong and tell her that everything is going to be okay. She also said that her partner must love dogs. I don't think this has to be a requirement in every marriage, but you must have mutual interests to have harmony in the marriage.

My next friend I have only known for a few months. However I thought it would be interesting to include her thoughts. **Anne** has just celebrated her forty-ninth birthday. She is a computer consultant and flies to different cities teaching computer software classes. She is very much a professional and is very intelligent. She is on the road for three weeks a month. She has never been married; she came close one time, but it wasn't right for her. It was very interesting to interview her on her thoughts of what she wants in a marriage. The first thing is 100 percent trust. With her being on the road as much as she is, I can understand that this has to be high on the list. She also wants security: financially, emotionally, and physically. She lives alone, and when on the road she is in and out of hotels. She wants companionship. While being single for so long, she says it is nice to have someone to do things with. She wants a feeling of warmth, comfort, and lots of laughter—someone she can let her guard down with. I think all too often we wear masks to keep people from seeing behind the mask. She wants someone to love her for who she is without trying to change her. She wants someone that is a mirror image of her, only better. She wants someone who makes her want to be a better person.

As you read through these responses, you find some common characteristics. All of these women want some of the same things; they just state it in different ways. Their ideals all have some of the same threads woven through them. A lot of their ideals are molded by their backgrounds. One of the common themes is honesty. No one wants to be lied to or to live with someone who is living a lie. Another theme is security: financially, emotionally, and physically. I believe that men can make a difference in this area. Husbands need to make their wives feel secure in the marriage. They need to know that their husband will be there to protect them and to provide for them and the children. Another theme is commitment. Women desire commitment to the family and the marriage; they want commitment for the long haul. They want someone who is going to be there through the good and the bad times that life throws at the family.

Women also want someone who is non-judgmental. They want someone that they can be themselves with, someone with whom they can let their guards down. Someone they can take their mask off with. They want someone who can see through the mask without ridiculing them. If a man has his eyes on the world this may be hard for him to do. If a man wants a supermodel or goes by the world's standards, he might find this hard to accept. The world tells us that we want the supermodel that acts like the mom in *Leave it to the Beaver*. Men want women to be perfect in every way without fault. In the meantime, we men are overweight and not the perfect husbands that we could be. Let's be honest: over time we all put on a few extra pounds and we don't dress the same way we used to (men and women). All that women want is someone who will cherish and honor them.

They desire someone who will put them before themselves, who will put them on a pedestal and enjoy being with them. They want someone who will lead them and give direction for the family.

Most men don't do this very well. Most men have jobs like me, where they are leaders at work. When we come home, we are tired of leading and want to let somebody else lead for a while. We want playtime. Remember, we are only thirteen. Men should be the head of the household and lead by example, God's example. They should lead with the consideration of the spouse and the family.

Lastly, women want someone who makes them feel good about themselves. They need someone that accepts them for who they are. Women need to feel pretty; they need to know that their men still desire to be with them. Women need to feel desirable; they need to know that they can still make their husbands' hearts skip a beat when they walk in the room. They need to know their husbands are thinking about them.

If you boil it all down, what women want in a marriage is:

A fearless leader who will fight for the woman he loves

Chivalry is not dead and may be the key to a long and happy marriage. Chivalry means treating the woman you love in a way she needs to feel loved. Remember that God put you together in this marriage. Do you want to mistreat the gift that God has given you? God has given you the most valuable thing in your life, why would you not honor and cherish it like the thing of beauty that it is? It is like a small seedling that is planted next to a stream. It needs nourishment, love and care. Women need men that will stand up for them, even when they are wrong. Women are the weaker sex. These are not my words; these are God's words.

1 Peter 3:7 "Husbands, likewise, dwell with them with understanding, giving honor to the wife, as to the weaker vessel, and as being heirs together of the grace of life, that your prayers may not be hindered."

My intention for this chapter is for both spouses to read this chapter. Men will be saying look at this while pointing out sections. The women also will be pointing to sections. What I hope will happen after this section is read by both is there is a time of reflection and a time that the spouses and sit down and openly discuss the section. A time that both spouses can be honest with each other. A time to discuss their marriage, and what they both would like for the marriage to look like. No mask no outside influences, just a time to come together. Some couples will say "yep we are on the right track and are the couple that God intended us to be. Some will take a different turn and Say "Wow I never knew that is how you felt". Take time to discuss this. It is important.

The Healing Process

This chapter has taken a huge turn for me over the last few months. God has allowed me to observe some things that I had not thought possible. Previously, my thoughts of marriage came from the Bible: marriage is until death.

1 Corinthians 7:10, 11 "Now to the married, I command yet not I but the lord: A wife is not to depart from her husband. But even if she does depart, let her remain unmarried or be reconciled to her husband. And a husband is not to divorce his wife."

Just like the vow, we stood up in front of my family, friends, and God and took a vow when my wife and I got married. I felt that you should work through the problems without giving up. However, over the last few weeks, God has allowed me to observe a time to call it quits and throw in the towel. Your safety and the safety of your kids is the most important thing. If there is abuse in the marriage, whether physical or emotional, you need to get out until the abuse is under control by a professional. The marriage needs to be put on hold until the abuse stops. This can only be done through professional help. This should be followed by a long period of time without abuse. This is true for mental illness and drug abuse as well. No marriage can be healthy and happy in these situations. Realizing this goes against my belief for many years. God has allowed me to go into a household controlled by mental illness. The person was self-medicating on alcohol. The living conditions in the home were very unsanitary. Trash was being stored in one of the bedrooms. We counted over three hundred gallon-jugs of alcohol mixed into the trash. No one deserves to live like this. The person had a mental illness and was very controlling. I know this sounds extreme, but it could be happening next door. People hide this very well in the fear of being found out. These kinds of problems can only be dealt with by a professional. If this sounds likes someone you know, or if it hits home, you must get help to get out of this situation. It doesn't get better on its own. Get professional help immediately.

More than half of married couples today have had thoughts of divorce or have envisioned themselves as being divorced. Most people who think about divorce have a shaded view of the pain that it causes. They don't have a clear view of the pain and hurt that is far-reaching. A lot of this pain comes with scars that are lifelong not only for them, but for the others involved as well. They have a very selfish view of things and are not taking into account the effects the divorce will have on others.

One of the pastors on TV preached a sermon on hurting people. He said that one in three people are hurting.

How many people do you work with? How many people do you pass on the way to work? How many of your friends are hurting? How many people do you encounter on a daily basis? How many are in your life/group/Sunday school class? The truth is there are a lot of people around you that are hurting, including some of you. What can you do to help ease their pain? Most of the time all people need is someone to listen to them. They need to be heard. Don't offer solutions—just listen and tell them that you will be praying for them. If they ask for direction, give them your thoughts. If they don't ask, don't try to give them lots of elaborate solutions: just listen to them. Can you take a few minutes to talk to them? They just need to be heard. You must be able to keep the conversation in confidence. If you can't, don't listen.

I have gotten a little off track here, but there are two ways of responding to emotional pain. You can wallow in self-pity, and complain that this pain is too great. Or, you can decide to change for the better. The difference in the two responses is perspective. It is all how you look at the problem. It is how you allow yourself to deal with the pain. Here are three ways to deal with pain:

1. Identify the pain. What caused it and what is the root of the pain?

2. Share the pain. Find someone you can trust and talk about the pain and how it makes you feel.

3. Allow God to heal the pain. Take it to God in prayer and allow him to comfort you through this pain.

God doesn't allow our hurt to go unused. Even though you can't see that while you are going through this pain, you will be able to use this experience to help someone else down the road. You will have a common bond with them and be able to know the pain they are feeling. I feel this is part of the reason God has allowed me to write this book. It has helped me put my thoughts and feelings on paper in order to help others in similar situations. It kind of makes all of the pain I went through bearable.

There are a few questions I want you to ask yourself:

1. What have you done to try to save your marriage?

2. What will you do to try to save your marriage?

3. What would you change to save your marriage?

Let's explore these questions.

1. **What have you done to try to save your marriage?**
   Hopefully you want to save your marriage. Hopefully
   you have tried several things to keep it intact. You know
   the definition of insanity is doing the same thing over
   and over expecting different results. You need to open
   your ears and listen to what your spouse wants and
   expects. Anger and bitterness are byproducts of unmet
   expectations. Find out what your spouse's expectations
   are and work to meet them.

2. **What will you do to save your marriage?** You
   need a plan. As stated above, you need to find out your
   spouse's expectations and then form a plan to meet
   them. This could even be something you sit down and
   talk about together. Identify the problem and then
   form a plan to overcome it. This is nothing more than

a problem-solving matrix that is used in businesses on a daily basis. The next step it to evaluate the plan to see if it is working. If the plan is not working change the plan or form a new plan.

3. **What would you change to save your marriage**? Everyone has limits to what they will do or put up with. What are your limits? I hope your limits are very high and there is not a lot you wouldn't do to save your marriage. I once told a friend of mine that he needed to do whatever it took to keep his marriage together, even if it meant dressing up as a chicken and holding a sign in front of her work that said "I love my wife."

You need a whatever-it-takes mentality. It takes a lot to get to this point: it takes commitment. It takes devotion. It takes the ability to keep going and trying new or different things to achieve your goal. It takes the ability to keep trying over and over. It takes a mind-set that failure is not an option. You have to get it in your heart that nothing is impossible. The key to success here is not the plan you create, but the help you receive in order to carry out your plan. There is only one healer and that is Jesus Christ. He is the one person you must have behind you to make this all happen. Before you start down any path of healing, you need him by your side. You need to spend time in prayer with him.

Even if your prayer is, "I don't know what to do; please help me," he will hear you. He will help guide you. He will give you strength to try one more time. He will give you comfort through the long and often bumpy path that it takes to reach your goal. He will show you the path to heal your marriage.

If you find yourself in a marriage that is hurting or has been weakening, here are a few steps to help you start the healing process. This process can be done as many times as necessary to reach your goal.

1. The first thing you need to do is to ask God to lead you down the path that will help heal the wounds that have formed.

2. The next step is to think about the problems that are present. Think about the expectations of your partner and your expectations.

3. The next step is to plan some time away together. This can be a weekend or just an overnight stay. It can be done in one day, but the process might be rushed and you may not achieve a good result. You can go to the next town or to the beach or to the mountains. It doesn't really matter where you go: the main focus is getting

away from distractions and focus on each other, allowing yourselves the time and space to fall in love again.

4. You need time to reconnect and refocus your marriage. No, it can't be done with the kids. Think of it like this: by spending some time away from your kids, you are giving them the gift of the good example of a happy marriage.

5. The next thing to do is to share your ground rules for your time away. For example: no loud talking and no arguing. This is time to work through and identify the problem. Don't fight about old stuff. This is a line in the sand, a new beginning. The past is the past. Some people have a hard time putting the past in the past. If this is the case, listen to them and tell them you are sorry and that this is the new beginning. Don't argue back. Don't point any fingers or try to place blame. You both will have to believe that this is a fresh new start for this to work. Get out a piece of paper and start working on identifying the problems. The list may be long at first. Once the list is done, take a break and stop for a few minutes. During this break, hug each other and tell your spouse that you love her. Then, come back to the list and try to condense it. Several of the problems will be similar and can be grouped together.

6. The next step is to start working on solutions. Try to get to the root of the problem before you try to solve the symptoms. Example: the husband might say that the problem is a lack of sex. However, the root of the problem may be that the wife is overworked and doesn't get enough help with the kids and is tired most of the time. The quick solution may be to make time for more sex, but the solution to the larger problem is to help your wife around the house. Perhaps you could give her some spa time to get her nails done. For a special treat. Don't be quick and rush through these problems: be sure to get to the root. This will increase the success of the whole process. Don't be afraid to ask *why* something is a problem. The answer may be very complicated, but work through it to get to the bottom. You may only work on one problem at a time. It may take several conversations before you address all the problems on your list, but remember the whatever-it-takes mentality. Trust me: everyone will be happier in the long run if you take time and work through the problems now. While you are away, take your spouse out to the best restaurant that your budget will allow. Alcohol should be kept to a minimum or not allowed at all. You need a clear head and you need to focus on the process. Keep in mind why you are here. You need to use this time to focus on each other. You need to be thinking about your

spouse, about what will make the experience better for him or her.

7. The next morning, you should focus on how the problems can be overcome and what behaviors are needed to make this work.

8. The last thing that needs to happen is a recommitment to the marriage. This can take many forms—it can be as simple as pledge to each other to make your marriage work, or it can be as elaborate as restating your vows to each other. This could be in a public ceremony or just standing face to face. You must write your vows down: you need them in front of you before you speak them to one another. Look each other eye to eye and say them. Yes, there will be tears streaming down your faces, but read through the tears. The husband and wife can make the same vows, or they can choose different ones. The original ones can be used or make new ones. The whole idea is that the line in the sand stays there: restating your vows puts the line in concrete. This will solidify your commitment to each other. This is a fresh start, a new beginning (the whatever–it–takes mentality).

Some people get caught up in negativity and choose to camp out there. Here is an exercise that will prevent you from doing that—it helps you focus on the positives and not dwell on the negatives. Pretend that your spouse has just been chosen to receive an award for best mother/father at your child's school. Your task is to write the award speech. Keep in mind as you write that you want to honor your spouse in front of your peers as well as your children. You wouldn't write something that indicated the honor was not warranted. You wouldn't want the children to feel that their parent was not the best in the world.

The healing process is a long and full of challenges. The process may need many treatments. Remember, the road to recovery is often just a set of goals. Once you meet your initial goals, you will reevaluate them and set new goals. This is the road to recovery. Think of someone who has had a major illness or accident. The first goal may be simply to stand. The next goal may be to take a few steps. After a while, the goal may be to walk again. This takes strength and courage. This is the same as the road to healing and recovery in a marriage. The road is paved with hurt and pain, but it is worth it in the end. It can be hard to see the end at times because you are still working toward the next step. I pray that God will give you focus to stay on the road, and that you achieve your goals. Sometimes it is hard to see the light at the end of the tunnel, but you've simply got to keep looking for it. As you get closer to your goal, the light will become brighter and clearer. God is an amazing healer and can heal your marriage if you will let him. Pray for commitment and direction while you are on the road to healing. God will fill the road with love, compassion, and strength to help you and your spouse finish the task.

Stopping the Epidemic

This is a huge task, a large goal. At the same time, you must believe it is possible. Nothing is impossible with God's help. If there were a medical disease that caused as much pain and suffering as divorce, people would be out in the streets crying for a cure. Think of the devastation of cancer, only worse. The disease of divorce affects more than half the families in America. It will have lasting effects on the children of many generations. *It must be stopped!*

You might be thinking, "Cute buzz words, but how do we stop divorce?" How can we rid America of this terrible disease? How can we stop the devastating effects it has on society? This disease has such a ripple effect that we don't yet fully understand its impact on society. My town was hit by a tornado that damaged or destroyed over two hundred homes. The region came together and helped these families in their time of need. My town has approximately 65,000 people. The tornado affected less than 2 percent of our town's population, yet the whole region came to help. I volunteered my time to helping the families affected. But think of the devastation that is caused by divorce. Divorce destroys half of our community's homes. Where is the help for them? As of this writing, I know of four families going through a divorce. These families are being destroyed. Why? When is this going to stop?

Think of a still pond. When you throw a rock in it, what happens? It causes a ripple effect. The ripple is more intense closer to the area of impact and has less of an effect the further out you go. The people closer to the divorce are affected the most and the people further away feel less of an effect. Now, pick up a handful of rocks and throw them into the pond. What happens? The ripples are all over the place, and each ripple is affected by the other ripples, and the area closet to the impact is in turmoil. This is the state we are in now. Nothing is safe from the ripples. We've got to stop the epidemic.

Like most men, I am a fixer. If it is broken, let's fix it. Once we have identified the problem, the only step is to fix the problem. But there is no easy fix for divorce, no magic pill, and no magic wand you can wave and make it all go away. It would be great if there were an easy way to ease our suffering, but there isn't.

Here is my solution: I think we need a three-prong attack. We need to hit the enemy hard and long. We need to stay with it till the threat is gone away. The three prongs are emotional, physical, and spiritual.

Emotional: People need to be healed emotionally. All too often, we hold on to grudges and hurt feelings. This turns into bitterness and revenge. We have got to let go of the pain. We need to identify the pain, draw a line in the sand, and let it go. Once we recognize the pain, it is up to us to determine how to live with it. Do we allow it to rule over us and affect your emotions? This will surely build resentment and bitterness. Do we recognize it and work on letting it go? Most of the pain in marriages comes from unmet expectations. We are our worst enemy. Can we be doing things that are causing our own pain? Sometimes our moral compass needs realigning. When our priorities become unaligned, we need to adjust them. This will keep things that don't belong, like selfness and laziness, out of our marriages. If we realign our moral compass and set our priorities back on the right path, we will strengthen our marriages and not break them down. This will help the pain not to rule our lives. This will take us back to the right path and set our course to get the rest of our lives in order. We have to start with ourselves first. If we aren't on the right path, it makes it hard for others to love us. It also makes it hard to accept the love of others. We need to love ourselves first before we can love others. Pain and bitterness keeps us from loving ourselves. Realign you priorities and set yourself on the right course. If you don't love yourself, how can you accept the love of others?

Physical: Physically, what can you do to improve your marriage? First, you need to exercise. Not only does this strengthen your body, it strengthens your mind. While you are walking or exercising, you are relaxing your mind. You are taking a mental break. Music will help you as you exercise. Far too many times I have been so relaxed I forgot what was even playing on the headphones. Mental breaks are essential to relaxing. I think we allow life to get in the way too much. We are way too busy. We sign our kids up for way too many activities, and we don't take time to sit down and relax. We let other things run our lives. Husbands, what would it look like if our wives were relaxed and full of energy? How can we be more relaxed ourselves? The home should be our sanctuary—places where we can let the worries of the day fade away, even if just for a few minutes. Relaxation could be time sitting on the porch. A relaxing bubble bath works for many women. No kids, no worrying about tomorrow, just plain old soaking in the tub. Whatever it is we choose to do, we all need time to unwind from our fast-paced world.

One source of trouble in our marriages is that we make time for everyone else except ourselves or our spouses. We need to slow down. Relationships are nothing more than spending time with another person. The more time you spend with a person, the stronger the relationship becomes. This is also true with our relationship with God. The more time we spend in prayer and reading his Word, the stronger our relationship with him becomes. If you have a good relationship with him, you will have a good relationship with your spouse. He can teach you many things. He can teach men to be men—to stand up and care for their wives. He can teach women how to love and care for their husbands. The Bible is full of marriage tips. A marriage is a relationship that completes us and not one that competes with us. Jesus said two shall become one. One body, one mind, and one soul. Look at **Matthew 19:5** and **Mark 10:8**. In most bibles the red words are what Jesus himself said.

Let's face it: you are not perfect. You have strengths and weaknesses, and you need a relationship to help improve your weaknesses. Your spouse will do just that. How can two become one if you are like two ships in the night, passing each other in the driveway? Slow down and take time for yourself and make time for each other. Who is the most important person in your life? Someone once said that life is like a pie. You give a slice to your kids, work, and other activities. If you don't have a slice for yourself at the end of the day, you become starved and malnourished. Have you ever been extremely hungry? All you can think about is food. You will go around looking for it everywhere until you find it. This sounds like selfishness, and it's the killer of most marriages.

Spiritual: First and foremost, you need a relationship with Jesus Christ. Second, you need to be in a church that focuses on scripture. Hopefully they will encourage you to read the Bible, which is something only 3 percent of people do on a regular basis. Remember: religion is manmade. The only thing that has stood the test of time is God's Word. Methodist, Catholic, and Baptist denominations are all man–made. I think the church as a whole has done a very poor job of strengthening marriages. In some ways, they have contributed to the weakening of the family. Yes, these are strong words and I am sure to offend someone. However, people often take time away from the family to attend functions of the church, such as meetings and other activities. I don't mean to suggest that these are unimportant or unnecessary, but some people allow their involvement to get out of hand and think that every time the church doors open, they need to be the ones opening them. Sometimes people allow the church and doing "good work" to get in the way of their marriage. Don't forget about the damaging effects of the political silliness that takes place in some churches. Does it really matter what color the carpet is? Does it matter what someone wears to church? I could go on and on about some of the silliness I have seen in churches, but does God really care about these things? Okay, I will get off my soapbox now. I think churches have the greatest potential to stop the divorce epidemic, if they would only quit fighting and backstabbing each other, return to the basics, and start strengthening the family. They need to make the strength of a marriage a top priority in the church. They need to pull together and stop this epidemic. There is only one God. People just worship him in different ways. I think churches get caught up in life and doing programs. They have lost the focus. I think church's need to foster the growth and strength of marriages. They need to help, not hurt, the family. Imagine what a church would look like if all the families in the church had strong marriages. Just the idea gives me goose bumps. If we had men who acted like men at the head of the household paired with women who completed their husbands, we would be able to put a stop to the epidemic. We would turn this city, state, and nation on its head. We could put a stop to the pain running rampant through or nation. We could stop the devastation of families and lives.

We can do it!!

We can stop the epidemic. We can strengthen marriages. We can change lives for the better. It takes commitment to make it work, and it takes a few steps. We are close to a cure. If we would realize this if we could only wake up and be the husbands and wives that we need to be. It takes commitment to have a healthy, strong marriage. We can have vibrant marriages—it can be done. It will work. I hope this book has given you some the strength to try one more time. I hope it has given you some ideas that will help you have the marriage that you deserve. I hope you have some ideas to survive the epidemic. I hope this has given you a vision of how life could be if we just put a little effort into our relationships. Divorce has got to stop. It is got to stop destroying the families. Make it work. Don't let life get in the way of a healthy marriage; take time to strengthen the marriage. Take time to have a strong marriage. Take time to create a good home for your children and grandchildren.

www.Stopping-divorce.com has been built to have a place for your ideas and feedback. This is also a place where you the reader can submit ideas to help strengthen marriages. I don't have all of the answers, but as a group we do. The site has a page of ideas of things to do to show your spouse you care. A playbook of sorts. Low or no cost ideas that help foster strength in a marriage.

On another page you will find consequences of divorce. This too has been submitted by readers. These struggles are placed there to help people see the far reaching affects that come from divorce. Effects not often thought of in the heat of the battle. Struggles, if evaluated, over a period of time, may help the reader think a little harder. Hopefully by the grace of God, these will help the reader make a better decision and try one more time to make the marriage better.

Whatever it takes!

About the Author

I grew up in central Georgia. Married at the age of sixteen and dropped out of high school to provide for my family. I worked in the textile industry while I finished high school at night and went on to Emergency Medical Technician School. After graduating, I began my career as a firefighter/ EMT. I later went on to Paramedic School and cross trained as a fireman. Today I am a Battalion Chief, having worked my way through the ranks. I have one daughter who has given me two wonderful grandchildren. After thirty years of marriage we divorced. I was fifteen years old the last time I had dated. I found myself alone, wondering what had happened. As I began to reflect on the past thirty years, I thought of different ways to do things. I began putting my thoughts down on paper. I found it helpful and somewhat healing to do this. After having your heart ripped to shreds, it was the only place I could focus my attention without being sad. A year after my divorce, God lead me to start forming this book, a small, simple way to help others avoid my path. The pain of divorce shines through this book. My hope is that this book, with God's help, will help readers avoid pain. If we can keep one marriage from divorce, we can slowly turn the tide of the epidemic that is plaguing the nation we know and love.